DISCARD

W9-BXE-809

THE CHILEAN
MINERS'
RESCUE

The Chilean

R Miners' Rescue

BY MARCIA AMIDON LUSTED

Content Consultant
Dr. Christopher J. Bise, chair of mining engineering
West Virginia University

ABDO
Publishing Company

CREDITS

Published by ABDO Publishing Company, 8000 West 78th Street, Edina, Minnesota 55439. Copyright © 2012 by Abdo Consulting Group, Inc. International copyrights reserved in all countries. No part of this book may be reproduced in any form without written permission from the publisher. The Essential Library™ is a trademark and logo of ABDO Publishing Company.

Printed in the United States of America,
North Mankato, Minnesota
062011
092011

Editor: Paula Lewis
Copy Editor: Rebecca Rowell
Cover Design: Kazuko Collins
Interior Design and Production: Marie Tupy

Library of Congress Cataloging-in-Publication Data
Lusted, Marcia Amidon.
   The Chilean miners' rescue / by Marcia Amidon Lusted.
      p. cm. -- (Essential events)
   Includes bibliographical references and index.
   ISBN 978-1-61783-097-6
   1. San Jose Mine Accident, Chile, 2010. 2. Mine accidents--Chile--Copiapo Region--Juvenile literature. 3. Mine rescue work--Chile--Copiapo Region--Juvenile literature. 4. Copper mines and mining--Accidents--Chile--Copiapo Region--Juvenile literature. 5. Gold mines and mining--Accidents--Chile--Copiapo Region--Juvenile literature. I. Title.
   TN311.L87 2012
   363.11'90983--dc23
                                      2011015027

The Chilean Miners' Rescue

TABLE OF CONTENTS

The entrance to the San José copper and gold mine near Copiapó, Chile

No Way Out

On the morning of August 5, 2010, miner Dario Segovia performed a job known as fortification in Chile's San José copper and gold mine. He attached metal nets to the roof of the mine to catch loose rocks and fragments that might fall onto miners and vehicles. Segovia said,

> *Before eleven a.m., I knew the mine would fall, but they sent us to place the reinforcement nets. We knew the roof was all bad and it would fall. It was dangerous; the roof was so fragile.*[1]

At 2:00 in the afternoon, the ground rumbled near the mine that was located in the Atacama Desert near Copiapó, Chile. Moments later, the mine's owner, the San Esteban Mining Company, realized a section of tunnel had collapsed deep inside the mine. One group of men who had been working near the mine's entrance escaped. Another group of 33 miners, however, were now trapped deep inside the mine. The three miles (5 km) of tunnels zigzagged from the mine entrance until they were approximately 2,300 feet (700 m) deep. There was no alternate way out.

A Small Accident

Lillian Ramirez, wife of miner Mario Gomez, had tried to convince her husband to stay home on August 5. Unaware of the collapse, she heard what she thought was the sound of her husband's truck returning home at 8:00 p.m. Instead of her husband, it was his boss. He told her there had been a small accident at the mine, which would be resolved the next day. Ramirez's nephew drove her to the mine that night. She would not return home again for months.

This was the beginning of a 69-day ordeal for the men trapped inside the San José mine and for those who endeavored to rescue them or waited for their safe return. As news of the mine collapse spread through the world's news media, no one knew if any of the 33 men had survived.

COPPER DEPENDENT

Chile is located along the western coast of South America on the Pacific Ocean. The Andes Mountains run almost the entire length of Chile on the east side. The Atacama Desert is in northern Chile between the ocean and the mountains. It is the driest desert in the world.

Northern Chile has a wealth of minerals, including copper, gold, silver, and nitrates, which are used in fertilizers and explosives. Chile leads the world in copper production and export. The nation is dependent on the profits from the sale of copper, which comprises one-third of its revenue. In 2010, Chile's copper export revenue rose 43 percent to approximately $39 billion. With its revenue from copper, Chile is the most prosperous country and a major economic power in South America.

THE FIRST ATTEMPTS

After the initial collapse, mine officials sent a search party into the access tunnel of the mine. No one really knew what had happened so far below the surface. Proceeding cautiously, the search party noticed cracks running through the walls, ceiling, and floor of the main tunnel. The searchers made it only 1,300 feet (396 m) into the tunnel before finding it blocked by a huge slab of rock. This confirmed the rescue of the 33 men would be difficult, if not impossible. André Sougarret, who headed the initial rescue operation at the mine, rode the

A Difficult Environment

Working in a mine is unhealthy business. Miners routinely suffer from respiratory infections caused by breathing in toxic particles of fine rock fragments. Some miners work in mines for decades, and their lungs become filled with debris. They often need to use medication to help their lungs function. In addition to the dust they breathe in, they are exposed to carbon monoxide fumes from vehicles and dynamite explosions. Paramedics assigned to a mine are frequently called to assist miners with breathing problems. Usually, the paramedics administer oxygen and take the miners to a hospital for a stay of several days.

At the time of the San José mine collapse, medical calls due to accidents and injuries were common. Many of the men who were trapped underground were overweight or addicted to drugs or alcohol and not in optimum health. The dust from the collapse, as well as the lack of fresh air, created a difficult situation for anyone still alive in the mine. It would be particularly difficult for those whose lungs were already compromised.

first rescue truck into the mine tunnel. He said, "We knew it collapsed. What does collapsed mean? What we found was a block, a tombstone, like when you're in an elevator and the doors open between floors."[2]

A Call for Help

As news of the mine collapse spread, Chileans were concerned about the 33 men and their families. On February 27, 2010, just six months earlier, Chile had experienced a major earthquake and tsunami. The government had been criticized for how it handled these disasters. Now, with this newest crisis, the government was under pressure to improve its responsiveness—and ensure the miners had every chance at survival. On August 6, the National Emergencies Office of the Interior Ministry released the names of the 33 trapped men. Thirty-two of the men were Chilean; one man was

A Leader

San Esteban, the company that owned the mine, should have been responsible for the rescue operation. Chile's president quickly understood the mining company did not have the manpower or the tools to lead the rescue and declared that the Chilean government would step in. The president then turned to Laurence Golborne.

With a degree in civil industrial engineering and a background in business management, Golborne had become Chile's mining minister less than five months before the mine collapse. Now he would lead the effort to rescue the 33 miners.

Golborne spoke with relatives of the trapped miners on August 7, 2010.

Bolivian. Laurence Golborne, Chile's minister of mining, returned from a visit to Ecuador to lead the rescue.

An Educated Man

In 1971, Piñera graduated at the top of his class in a Chilean university as a commercial engineer. In 1973, he earned a doctorate in economics from Harvard University in Cambridge, Massachusetts. He saw firsthand how the concepts of freedom and democracy worked in the United States.

By 1988, he actively worked to end the military regime in Chile so the nation could once again be a democracy. Over the next few years, he was an economics professor, a businessman, and a senator.

Piñera ran for president in 2005 but lost. He continued to travel across Chile and listened to the needs of the people. He created 37 commissions to research and propose public policies.

Once again, in 2009, Piñera became a presidential candidate. On March 11, 2010, just five months before the San José mine collapsed, Piñera was elected Chile's president.

News of the disaster quickly reached the outside world. Chilean President Sebastián Piñera used his business contacts and the diplomatic communication channels between countries around the world to call for help. "We have these guys trapped at seven hundred meters [2,300 feet]. What technologies do you have that could possibly help?"[3] The president received an overwhelming response. Engineers, rescue workers, drillers, and diggers came to the remote mine to volunteer their time, labor, and ideas.

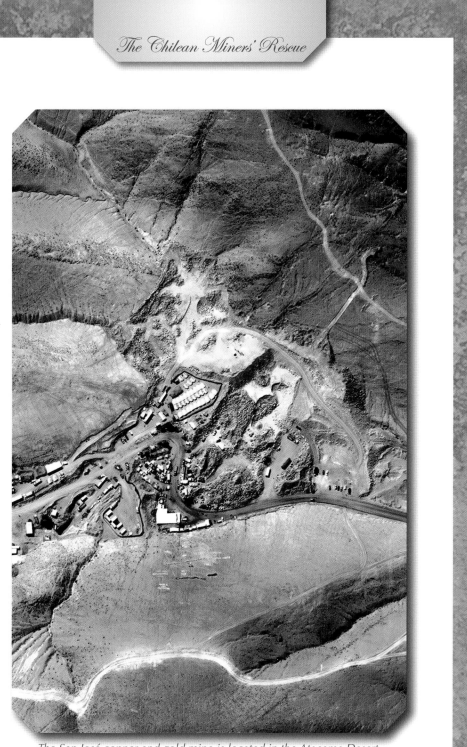

The San José copper and gold mine is located in the Atacama Desert.

The entrance to a copper mine in a mountain

THE SAN JOSÉ MINE

Opened in 1889, the small San José mine produced copper and gold. To find every trace of these valuable minerals, miners had created tunnels with sharp turns and angles that gradually led them deeper into the ground.

Because the mine had a reputation as the most dangerous in the region, its miners received higher wages than those who worked in other mines. The San Esteban Mining Company, which owned the mine, was known for its poor safety record. In the prior six years, three men had died in the San José mine. The road the miners traveled by bus to reach the mine site every day passed a small row of shrines to honor the men who had died suddenly and tragically in the mine. The shrines held lit candles, fresh flowers, and photographs. In the days following the August 5 collapse, shrines to the trapped miners would be added.

Known for its mining, Chile is the top producer of copper in the world. Most of the miners in Chile work in the northern deserts where the modern copper mines are equipped with the latest mining technology and operate as safely

One of Many Accidents

The San José mine was never known for following safety regulations. In 1985, Ivan Toro began working at the mine. Sneakers were the standard footwear for miners, rather than steel-toed boots or other types of safety footwear.

One day in 2001, as Toro waited for a truck to take him to the surface, a section of the mine's roof collapsed. He later said, "We could hear the machines perforating in the level above us when suddenly a slab of rock fell. I was the most affected because it fell on my leg. There were just little strands left and they amputated it."[1]

At first, the company refused to pay Toro any compensation because he had been sitting down and not working. Toro sued the mine and eventually was awarded approximately $45,000.

as a mine can operate. Jonathan Franklin, author of *33 Men: Inside the Miraculous Survival and Dramatic Rescue of the Chilean Miners*, stated,

> *Mining jobs are coveted as both lucrative and safe—considering that "safety" in the world of mining is relative. Combine the risks of young men driving truckloads of ammonium nitrate explosives, hundreds of miners setting dynamite charges inside caves every day, and all this taking place in Chile, a nation known to have the world's biggest earthquakes, and accidents are almost a certainty.*[2]

The San José mine, however, was not a modern, well-equipped mine. It was part of a more primitive class of mining in Chile. Work was done almost the same way the original miners, known as *pirquineros*, or artisan miners, once mined, using only donkeys and pickaxes. While the miners at San José used modern machinery inside the mine, the

A Survivor

On July 5, 2010, one month before the San José mine collapsed, the miners had witnessed a grisly accident. Miner Gino Cortez passed beneath a huge block of rock when it became loose and fell on his leg, severing it. The accident was so sudden that Cortez was not immediately aware his leg had been cut off. A coworker wrapped the leg in a shirt and took it to the hospital with Cortez, but the leg could not be reattached. Cortez, however, considered he was lucky to have survived the accident.

methods were not much different from the earlier days. As a result, miners were often crushed by large slabs of falling rock or scraped their skin on sharp rocks inside the mine. Many of the miners operated dangerous and complex machinery without training and were expected to learn on the job. Explosives were used in the underground caves almost daily. Safety procedures were minimal and accidents were common.

A Maze of Tunnels

People often envision a mine as having flat tunnels that bore directly into the

Dangers and Violations

The San Esteban Mining Company owned the San José mine, in addition to others. The company was known for its disregard of safety practices. In Chile, many medium and small mines were not closely regulated and could not afford to follow safety practices as closely as large companies.

The San José mine was one of the most dangerous places to work. The mine had been shut down by the government in 2006 and 2007 for not following safety practices. Between 2004 and 2010, the company received 42 fines for safety violations. Mining trade unions tried to shut down the mine again after several fatalities occurred, but it remained open—possibly due to bribes paid to government officials. Workers claimed all along that management made decisions about operating the mines without listening to their workers, who explained the dangers and risks. Because of its reputation for being dangerous and ignoring safety practices, the San José mine paid higher wages than other mines, making it attractive to workers. It also was willing to hire older workers who were grateful to have jobs and less likely to complain.

mountainside. But the San José mine was so old the mountain was honeycombed with tunnels—most of which spiraled downward into the ground like a giant, coiled spring. Because the mine was old, it had been excavated haphazardly. With so many tunnels and holes, some workers wondered how the roof stayed up. Support pillars had been carved into the mountain and were intended to be left in place every 160 feet (49 m). In the San José mine, those pillars also had been mined for copper and gold. After so many years of mining, the mine had very little support structure left.

In addition to the downward spiraling tunnels, the San José mine also had ventilation shafts, emergency escape routes, an underground repair workshop, and an emergency refuge or shelter. The shelter was approximately 2,300 feet (700 m) below the surface. Approximately 540 square feet (50 sq m) in size, it was stocked with oxygen, food, and drink to last 48 hours.

Modern copper mining in Chile is done in a large, open pit, and the largest open pit mine in the world is located in Chile. In the San José mine, however, miners drilled holes into the rock and placed sticks of dynamite in the holes to blast

The Chuquicamata open pit copper mine is in northern Chile.

the rock. The rock fragments were scooped up by
a loader and put into trucks to be hauled away. By
blasting away the rock, the miners hoped veins of
copper or gold ore would be revealed inside the
rock. Some copper mining involved crushing the

combination of rock and copper into tiny pieces and then using a chemical process to extract the copper.

Long Shifts and Harsh Conditions

Workers in the San José mine worked seven days and then had seven days off. Each shift was 12 hours. The men took a bus to the mine site and changed into work pants or shorts and a T-shirt. One practical safety measure was a helmet with a headlamp. Franklin Lobos, the official driver, drove deep into the mine, ferrying the men in a cargo truck. Each man carried water bottles. Because of the heat and dust, most of the workers drank approximately three quarts (3 L) of water a day, and even this was not enough to counteract the heat and humidity of the mine and the loss of body moisture through sweating. Due to the heat, some men worked wearing only their underwear and boots. The temperature was rarely cooler than 90 degrees Fahrenheit (32°C). Though the mine provided food for the men, many carried extra food. Because some foremen frowned on this as a distraction from work, men were known to hide the extra food in their clothing.

The air in the mine was heavy with rock dust, vehicle exhaust, and cigarette smoke. It was noisy with the rumbling of machinery, the explosions of dynamite, and the occasional creaks in the rock of the mountain. Most men wore ear protection and conversation was not possible. Many miners usually worked in small groups, but others often worked alone.

LAST MAN DOWN

On August 5, just after 1:00 p.m., Lobos began his drive down into the San José mine. He stopped his truck halfway down to talk to another driver and heard the mine crack. Jorge Galleguillos, who rode in the truck with Lobos, later wrote,

> *As we were driving down, a slab of rock caved in just behind us. It crashed down only a few seconds after we drove past. After that, we were caught in an avalanche of dirt and dust. I couldn't see my hand in front of my face. The tunnel was collapsing.*[3]

A Forewarning?

At 11:30 on the morning of the collapse, the mountain made a cracking noise. The San José miners asked Carlos Pinilla, the head of the mining operations, what was going on. He reassured them it was just a normal sound made by the mine settling and told them to stay deep in the mine and keep working. Pinilla then immediately took the first available vehicle and drove to the surface. One of the miners testified, "He left early that day and he never did that. He would usually leave at one or one-thirty and that day he left around eleven. He was scared."[4]

Layer after layer of the spiraling tunnel collapsed upon itself. Lobos managed to avoid the collapsing sections and descended to the refuge deep underground, which was designed to be a safe place to go in the event of a mine collapse. The miners knew this first crack was more than the usual small avalanches that occurred in the mine. The men took refuge and braced themselves for an explosion of air called the piston effect, which followed a collapse.

When a mine caves in, a forceful displacement of the air inside the cave occurs. This generates strong winds that push the miners up against the walls so hard their bones can break. Waves of dust and dirt are pushed down the tunnel, choking and blinding the men. According to Miguel Fortt, an expert in mine rescues in Chile, "A true piston effect is like an explosion. It is a deep sound, like a herd of galloping buffalo. You have very little time to react. You can't do much."[5] The force of the air eventually shot through the top of the mountain. Witnesses on the outside described it as a volcano exploding.

It took three hours for the dust to settle inside the mine. But it would be much longer before anyone on the surface knew the fate of the 33 miners.

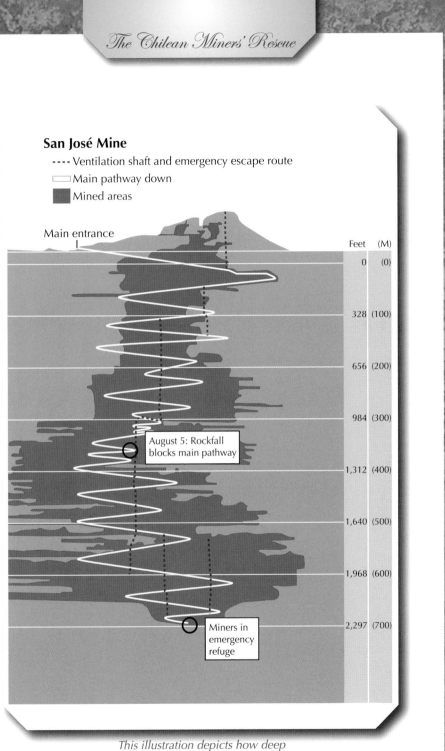

San José Mine

---- Ventilation shaft and emergency escape route

▭ Main pathway down

▮ Mined areas

Main entrance

| Feet | (M) |

0 (0)
328 (100)
656 (200)
984 (300)

August 5: Rockfall blocks main pathway

1,312 (400)
1,640 (500)
1,968 (600)

Miners in emergency refuge

2,297 (700)

*This illustration depicts how deep
the miners were trapped in the mountain.*

Not knowing the fate of the miners, family members gathered at the mine.

IS ANYONE THERE?

*I*t was almost 6:00 p.m. on August 5 when the Chilean Carabineros Special Operations Group (GOPE) received a call about a mining accident at the San José mine. This special police unit handled many kinds of rescue operations, including mountain climbing and ocean rescues. When the six men arrived at the mine, a geologist and a geophysicist were waiting with information. They did not have an accurate map of the mine but sketched out what they could for the rescue team. In the first attempt to reach the miners, rescuers drove a truck in as far as possible but found the tunnel blocked. The next suggestion was for the rescuers to use the ventilation shaft at the top of the mine. This would allow them to lower themselves inside the mine and search for survivors.

A national news bulletin was the first indication to the public that something had occurred at the mine. The mine authorities had not contacted the families of the missing miners. They also had not allowed miners on the surface to call police or firefighters. Wanting to handle the disaster on its own terms, it was hours before the mining company

GOPE

Chile's national police, the Carabineros, are responsible for border security, public safety, dismantling bombs, and crime and narcotics control. Similar to US military reserve units, the Carabineros can be called up by the Chilean army. At the time of the mine collapse, it was not clear if the GOPE team would be rescuing the men or finding their bodies.

realized it needed help and notified the authorities.

GOPE member Mario Segura was the first to enter the mine. He recalled,

> We went down into the mine and followed it as far as possible, and then we came to a spot where the road was blocked by debris and rock. Usually you find a way around the edges of a cave-in. But this was a smooth rock, like a door that sealed off the shaft. The way the mountain collapsed, even the experts in mining did not understand how much rock fell.[1]

Officials later estimated this piece of rock weighed 700,000 short tons (635,029 metric tons), approximately twice the weight of New York City's Empire State Building. When the GOPE team realized there was no way around the rock, they located one of the ventilation shafts and climbed down it using rock climbing equipment.

Missing Gear

The GOPE team had quickly packed their gear in the rush to reach the San José mine. In their haste, they forgot one vital piece of equipment—a tripod. Centered above a hole, a tripod helps rescuers descend on ropes by guiding the flow of the rope and keeping it from fraying on the sharp rocks. Without a tripod, the rescuers tied their rope to the bumper of a pickup truck. They had to yank the line to keep it away from the rocks as they descended through the ventilation shaft.

As they descended through the narrow shaft, the GOPE team looked for signs of life and called out for survivors. Segura knew the team "had to keep searching, but the sound of that mountain, it was like rocks screaming and crying."[2]

Another searcher, Lieutenant José Luis Villegas, commented,

> *We were all very anxious. We reached a lower level and we were a little upset that the tunnel was still blocked but that kept us going. We said, "No . . . the next one will be open." . . . and we kept on going down, but each level was [sealed off].*[3]

A Setback and a New Strategy

The searchers continued to enter several different tunnels and ventilation shafts but could not find a clear way to reach the trapped men. In an attempt to gain access to one of the ventilation shafts, heavy machinery was used, which triggered another collapse on day two, August 7. This landslide blocked the ventilation shaft, and now the GOPE team had to be rescued. The shafts could no longer be used for a possible rescue of the trapped miners.

On the same day, Golborne arranged for the first drilling rig to arrive at the mine. When Golborne told Piñera this, the Chilean president responded, "Okay, well done. Now I want you to get not just one but ten drilling rigs."[4] Piñera had decided that the best way to save the miners, if they were still alive, was to have as many rescue operations going simultaneously as possible. He used this strategy throughout the rescue process.

On August 9, Piñera appointed André Sougarret as the general manager of the rescue effort. As the manager of mines at Chile's state-owned El Teniente copper mine, Sougarret was an excellent choice to head the rescue effort at San José. He knew he had to find just the right spot in the layers of volcanic rock where the drills would reach the mine. Since the mine was poorly mapped, this was a difficult task. He also had to

Safety First

Safety regulations for mines mandate emergency shafts are to be equipped with ladders. These would allow miners to climb to safety in the event of a collapse or other emergency. The shafts at the San José mine did not have safety ladders. Many of the miners claim that if the ladders were in place, they could have climbed to safety in the first few hours of the collapse before the shafts were blocked by shifting rocks.

Copper is stacked up in El Teniente, which is the world's largest underground copper mine and managed by Sougarret.

work out contingency plans in case something went wrong. Because the mine was on a geologic fault, the difficulty in drilling was compounded.

Sougarret's first job was to organize all the drilling equipment the Chile mining community had sent to the mine site. Drilling machines capable of drilling through hundreds of feet of rock to create boreholes were of particular importance. The engineers knew it was too dangerous to attempt a rescue through the entrance of the mine because the mountain was unstable. Drilling six-inch (15-cm) boreholes with a 3.5-inch (9-cm) diameter drill bit was the fastest way to make contact with any miners who were still alive. Sougarret organized the different types of drill rigs to drill eight exploratory boreholes. Some drilled faster while others drilled more slowly and more precisely.

A Low Profile

Sougarret kept a very low profile during the mine rescue, allowing Chile's president and cabinet members to take leading roles while he worked in the background.

Hope Fades

By day seven, August 12, nine drills had reached a depth of approximately 1,640 feet (500 m), but no contact had been made. The drillers were aiming for the tunnels and the refuge deep within the mine, but it was almost impossible to drill accurately without precise maps of the mine. Golborne acknowledged the chance of finding anyone alive was low. Hope began to fade among the families of the miners and the rescue teams.

On August 19, the first borehole reached an area where the miners were believed to be trapped. Unknowingly, they were 80 feet (24.4 m) below the miners. The rescuers waited for any indication of the presence of the men but found no signs of life. It had been two weeks since the collapse, and no one knew if any of the men had survived. Some thought it was too late for a rescue attempt. Others thought there was little chance that any of the 33 men trapped 2,300 feet (701 m) below could be alive. Still others wondered if the men could ever be rescued. The miners' spirits sunk as they realized the drill had bypassed them. They now expected death instead of rescue.

By day 16, August 21, Borehole Ten B had reached approximately 2,100 feet (640 m), which should have put it less than 160 feet (49 m) from its target. However, the engineers running the drill rig also

Camp Hope

Word soon spread to the trapped miners' families, and they began streaming to the mine site. An area where the waste rock from the mining process was dumped became a windbreak. Family members set up shrines and created their own village of tents and trailers to stay close to the mine as they awaited word of their loved ones. This makeshift settlement was named Camp Hope. Eventually, the Chilean army brought in portable toilets and set up a field kitchen at Camp Hope, offering meals several times a day. Volunteers included family members of the miners and people who wanted to help.

knew the drill was slightly off course, despite efforts to keep it aimed correctly. Sougarret said, "We didn't have much faith that it would hit."[5] Time was running out for any men who might be trapped so deep in the mine, and the engineers knew they had only this one chance. A few more feet and they would most likely know if their rescue effort was in vain.

Drilling Rig

An oil-drilling rig was one of the methods rescuers used in their attempts to reach the miners. This type of rig consists of a power system—usually a diesel engine and auxiliary electric generators—a mechanical system to winch cables and drills in and out of the hole being drilled, and rotating equipment to drive the rotary drill.

Oil drills insert a concrete casing into the hole as it is drilled. In the case of the Chilean mine rescue, however, the casing came later and was used only in parts of the completed hole. Oil drill rigs have a circulation system to keep the drill bit lubricated and to remove mud and rock cuttings from the hole. The entire rig sits on a platform with a derrick that rises as much as 195 feet (59.4 m) into the air to hold the hoisting system. The drill usually consists of a bit with rotating heads, a drill string, and a drill collar. The drill string is made up of connected sections of drill pipe that is lengthened as the drill goes deeper. The collar fits around the drilling pipe to put weight on the drill bit. The various drill bits are made in different shapes and from a variety of materials, including tungsten steel, carbide steel, and diamond, depending on what type of rock is being drilled.

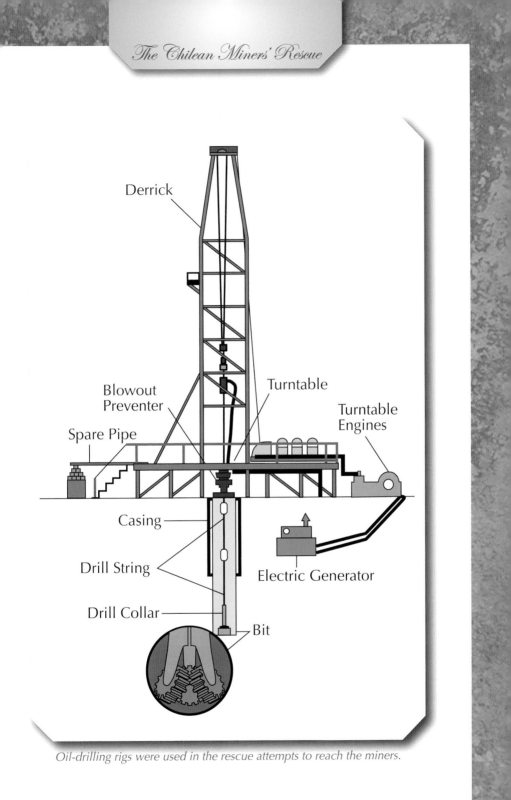

Derrick

Blowout
Preventer

Spare Pipe

Turntable

Turntable
Engines

Casing

Drill String

Drill Collar

Electric Generator

Bit

Oil-drilling rigs were used in the rescue attempts to reach the miners.

*Relatives at Camp Hope cheered upon learning a drill
had reached the depth where the miners were believed to be trapped.*

We Are Alive

On day 17, August 22, 2010, Nelson Flores was the lead operator of the drill making its way deep into the mine. Knowing he was close to breaking through into an open space, he slowed the drill at 2,165 feet (660 m). He wanted to break into the space with a clean hole. If the drill moved too fast, it might break through the rock and send shards of sharp rock into the space, injuring or killing anyone nearby. At 5:50 a.m., a small crowd gathered around the borehole. Everyone held their breath as the drill continued to run. Finally, Flores did not feel any resistance. The drill had reached empty space.

Flores shut down the drill. An assistant took a hammer and pounded the drill tube three times. Then he waited, pressing his ear to the tube. Eduardo Hurtado, a geologist on the team, drilled the first borehole. He mentioned he heard a faint tapping as though someone was hitting the tube with a spoon. But they had been fooled before with a different borehole, hearing a tapping but not seeing anything when a camera was sent down through the hole. But this time, someone was pounding on the tube.

"I was awake . . . the drill broke through, it was the most marvelous moment for all of us. We looked at the drill and were stunned. It even took us a few moments to understand the importance of what happened. Only then did we start to hug and celebrate. We then understood the reality. They were going to save us."[1]

—*Richard Villarroel*

Greg Hall, a mining engineer, recalled the moment:

On day 17, one of the rigs my technicians were working on found a void, which was good, and my technician called me and said, "Greg, we think we hear pounding on the drill pipe." And that's when I thought, "Well, maybe one or two of them survived." We tripped out the drill pipe, and in between our hammer and bit was [a] note. [2]

The note attached to the drill bit became famous. As the technician unwrapped the scrap of paper, written on it in clear red letters were the words "*Estamos Bien En El Refugio los 33*," which is Spanish for "We are all right in the shelter, the 33 of us." [3]

The note was read aloud. People celebrated; the engineers jumped up and down and hugged each other. A mining technician ran down the hill to Camp Hope, screaming the good news that all the miners were alive.

A Miracle

When the rescuers read the note from the miners, Hall said, "That was amazing. . . . such a miracle. Again, we were hoping one or two of them were alive. But to find out that all 33 men were alive was amazing." [4]

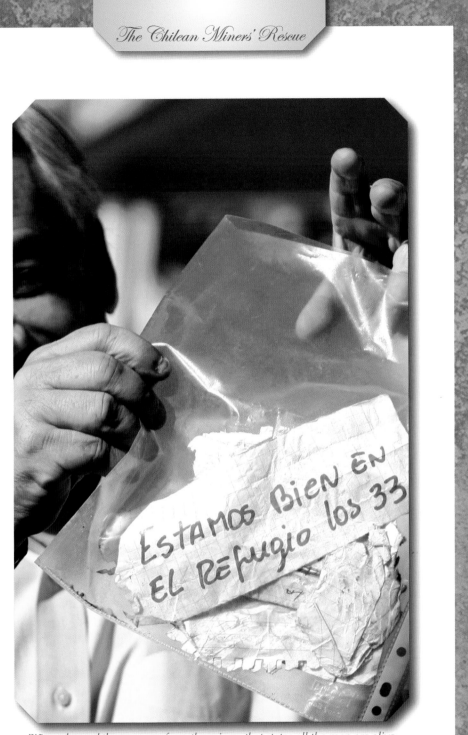

Piñera showed the message from the miners that states all the men are alive.

From Recovery to Rescue

A miracle had happened. The 33 men were alive deep underground. All around Chile, and then the world, the good news spread. Communication was established with the miners. Soon, food and other necessities would be sent down through the small boreholes. The mission at the San José mine had turned from one of recovering bodies to one of determining how to rescue 33 men from deep inside the earth.

The First Images

The next step was to send down a tiny remote-controlled video camera to the miners. It reached the floor of the space and unfolded. The first image sent back to the surface was

---

Leadership

Luiz Urzúa was the highest-ranking man among the 33 men trapped in the mine. As the shift foreman, he did not participate in the physical work of the mine. Instead, his job was to guide, motivate, and sometimes prod the men working on his shift. In the mine, the shift foreman is to be obeyed. A miner who did not obey the foreman's authority could be disciplined or dismissed.

The Chilean minister of health, Jaime Mānalich, explained the position of shift foreman by saying, "The world of natural selection functions quite strongly in this environment. To arrive at the position of shift foreman, you have to pass through many a test."[5] Although Urzúa had 20 years of experience in mining, he was new to the San José mine and some questioned whether he should be the group leader. During their time trapped underground, the leadership shifted, but Urzúa's actions are still credited with saving the men's lives.

of 54-year-old Luiz Urzúa, the shift foreman. He said, "If you can hear me, raise the camera."[6] Slowly the camera was raised and lowered. Twenty minutes later, the camera was pulled back to the surface. Journalist Franklin wrote:

> *The images broadcast back to [the rescuers] were eerie and hard to decipher. Dim lights shone in the background, obviously the head lamps of the miners who had crowded close to the camera. But the low light conditions made the resolution so grainy that the rescuers could only guess at the face they were seeing.[7]*

Two hours later, with a tent used as a screen, the first images of the men were shown to their families. That night, Camp Hope was filled with celebration. Juan Barraza, a local priest, said, "To know they were alive allowed everyone to express many emotions that had been held back. Now everyone was saying, 'We won't go home without them.'"[8]

Eyewitness Accounts

Eventually, the 33 men described their first days after the mine collapse. They had suffered eye irritation from the thick cloud of dust created by the falling slabs of rock. Still, they actively looked for a way out. Their first thought was to escape through the system of ventilation shafts, which should have been equipped with ladders for this type of circumstance. But the ladders were missing or in disrepair. The shafts became inaccessible when a second collapse crushed the shafts two days later.

The miners knew they were in a dangerous, life-threatening situation. Richard Villarroel later described those first hours. Franklin and Juan Forero, who interviewed him, wrote:

> Some of the men were so sure death was near that they simply climbed into cots in the cavern and would not get up. [Villarroel] described being overwhelmed with the dread of never again seeing his doting mother, Antonia Godoy, or meeting the boy his pregnant wife is carrying.[9]

Leadership

Urzúa, the shift supervisor, took action. He had sent his men to the refuge. This area was designed to be a safe place to go in the event of a mine collapse. Urzúa assigned roles to his men and sent the most experienced miners out to assess the damage and determine if they could find a way out. After taking stock of their canned foods and drinks, he rationed how much the men were allowed to eat and drink each day.

Urzúa understood that the men not only needed to remain healthy to survive, but they also needed to stay focused. He organized the underground space to include separate areas for working and sleeping. He knew the importance of a schedule and kept the men on 12-hour shifts. The headlights of the trucks in the mine simulated daylight.

But Urzúa was not the only leader to step forward. The oldest of the trapped miners, 69-year-old Mario Gomez, took on the role of spiritual guide during a time filled with fear and the unknown. Fifteen years earlier, Yonni Barrios had taken a nursing course. He called on those skills to dispense medicines and administer health tests that were sent through a borehole.

Many of the miners and rescuers acknowledged Urzúa's quick actions

A Refuge

The shelter, or refuge, deep in the mine was a small room. It had a ceramic tile floor and a reinforced ceiling. It contained two oxygen tanks—which the 33 men took turns breathing from after the initial dust cloud from the collapse. It also had a cabinet filled with old medicines and a small supply of food, including water, canned food, milk, juice, and crackers. The food was intended for an emergency for 10 miners over a period of 48 hours. With 33 men, the food needed to be carefully rationed to last as long as possible.

made it possible for the men to survive in those first few weeks. A UK newspaper, the *Guardian*, reported:

> *Immediately after the collapse at the mine at lunchtime on 5 August, Urzúa sent men to investigate. Some drove a pickup, inching up a ramp. With clouds of dust limiting visibility . . . they were unable to see the path and crashed. "We were trying to find out what we could do and what we could not," said Urzúa.*[10]

Urzúa's careful command of the situation paid off. His men were safe and had been found by the rescuers. Still, they knew it would take time. As they waited, the environment, the subgroups that had formed, and the miner's concerns took a toll on the men. Many of the men were superstitious and felt the mountain would not willingly release them.

No Compensation

The San Esteban Mining Company was not doing well financially. While the company could not fund the rescue operation, it also did not want the public to know that the company might go bankrupt. The miners did not receive compensation during the days they were in the collapsed mine.

The miners' union asked the government to pay the wages of the 33 miners as well as other San Esteban miners who were out of work. The government, however, claimed the labor laws did not allow for any compensation. Mining Minister Golborne suggested the government offer the miners training to find other jobs when they were rescued.

A small, remote-controlled camera was sent down to the trapped miners.

The Strata 950 drilling machine at the San José mine was part of Plan A.

Plan A

*N*ow that rescuers knew for certain the men in the mine were alive, they had to establish priorities. Their first concern was for the men's health and well-being. Getting them out of the mine was their second concern. Rescuers knew they could not rely on a single borehole for communication and sending supplies to the men, so they decided on three. One borehole would be used as a delivery chute for food and water. A second borehole would deliver oxygen, water, and electricity. The third borehole was intended to reach far away from the men's living quarters and might eventually be used to rescue the miners. Anything to be delivered to the men had to fit within the small 3.5-inch (9-cm) diameter tube—approximately the diameter of an orange.

The rescuers also knew the men would be in the mine for a long period of time. Any rescue was expected to take as long as four months.

Refeeding Syndrome

After surviving for weeks on very little food and contaminated water, the 33 miners were in precarious health. From the videos, it appeared that each man had lost approximately 20 pounds (9 kg).

The type and amount of food that was sent to the miners was carefully selected for two reasons. Full-size, solid meals could kill them. When a starving person is fed a large meal with lots of carbohydrates, it can start a chemical chain reaction that drains essential

*Water, food, and letters were passed to the miners
in tubes through the borehole.*

minerals from the heart. Known as the refeeding
syndrome, it leads to cardiac arrest—a heart attack—
and death. The other reason was the men needed to

be careful about their weight in order to fit in the rescue capsule.

WAITING FOR THE RESCUE

The miners might have dreamed of their favorite foods, but on August 23, the rescuers sent down food and nutrients to nurse the men back to health. Because the men had been starving, too much food at once could shock their bodies. At first, the men were given tiny doses of liquid glucose and allowed sips of bottled water at regular intervals. Medicine was also sent down. After 48 hours, the men were allowed to eat solid food.

On day 18, a tiny telephone with a fiber optic cable was sent down the tube, allowing the miners to speak to those on the surface. Golborne spoke to the men:

"Hello," said Golborne. "Yes, I hear you!" A rousing cheer and applause

A Generous Man

Leonardo Farkas, a Chilean businessman, owned several open-pit Chilean mining operations. Not only generous, he was conscientious regarding safety concerns. Miners were on waiting lists to work for his companies. Farkas arrived at the San José mine on day 18, August 23. He walked around Camp Hope and gave the family of each trapped miner a plain white envelope. Inside each envelope was a check for 10 million Chilean pesos, which is approximately $20,580. After the men were rescued, he gave each miner another 5 million pesos, approximately $10,590. At one point, he even talked of buying the mine so it could be closed forever.

erupted from the rescue workers, who quickly quieted to listen on speakerphone. A clear and calm voice was heard: "This is shift foreman Luis Urzúa. . . . We are waiting for the rescue."[1]

As the news of the men's survival spread around the world, the media flocked to this remote desert in Chile. Airplane flights and hotel rooms were impossible to find, the rental prices of motor homes soared, and translators were sought after. The story of the Chilean miners was in demand.

STRATA 950

The first of three plans for rescuing the trapped men was underway. Plan A involved a Strata 950 raise borer. This borer uses the grinding movement of three tungsten steel disks to drill a hole. The discs would be followed by a reamer to widen the hole. The plan was to create a tube 28 inches (71 cm) in diameter down to the miners and use a steel cage inside the hole to lift each man to safety.

Of the six Strata machines in the world, one was located in Chile. The machine could drill a hole as deep as two miles (3.2 km) at a cost of $3,000 to $5,000 for every 3.2 feet (1 m) drilled. The Strata machine would need 4.5 gallons (17 L) of water every second to lubricate the drill. In many places, this would not be a problem, but the San José mine was located in the middle of a desert. It would take convoys of tanker trucks to supply the water for the drill.

The downside of Plan A was that it would take approximately four months to finish the rescue tunnel. Many feared the 33 men might not be sane or even alive after that much time underground. Because this plan was slow and the rescue mission was such a complicated and challenging one, Piñera and his

Standing Vigil

As news of the mine disaster spread, family and media members began a vigil as they awaited news. Friends and families placed flags on the ridge—32 Chilean flags and a Bolivian flag for the one Bolivian miner.

Among the media and satellite trailers, family members had set up tents. Some of the wives and girlfriends were going through pregnancies, hoping their soon-to-be-born children would know their fathers. Children too young to understand played and asked questions.

Andreas Llarena, a navy physician, said:

They are not a bunch of tourists trapped in a cave. They are miners used to working underground, they know how the earth operates, this environment is not a mystery to them. They are trapped in the equivalent of their office. That's not a good situation, but it is a huge advantage.[2]

Two weeks after the mine collapsed, the burden of not knowing became more difficult for many. The mood of Camp Hope turned joyous when they learned of the message that had been sent up on the drill bit announcing all 33 men were alive in the mine's refuge.

"We are in uncharted territory here," acknowledged Dr. Rodrigo Figueroa, an emergency mental health specialist. "Nobody has ever had to go through what these men are experiencing."[3]

government decided to use more than one drilling plan at a time. But on day 26—August 31—Plan A was put into action.

Camp Hope

Camp Hope was growing. It now held 500 people and more arrived every week as the media arrived to tell the miners' story. Camp Hope had places for children to play, community bulletin boards, a shuttle bus service to area cities, and a stage where evangelists preached to the camp members. Food companies brought donations for the camp residents. Adolfo Duran, who worked for the dairy processor Soprole, said,

> We are here to provide support to the families and the kids. Every four or five days we bring milk and yogurt. . . . The feeling of fraternity has been augmented heavily this year; first we had the earthquake and now this. Personally, I feel like our nation had become much stronger this year.[4]

Rescue workers from all over the world gathered at the San José mine. Men from Brazil, South Africa, the United States, and Canada offered to help the Chilean rescue workers and volunteers. They worked 12-hour shifts to free men they did not know.

STRESS AND MORALE

However, the new ability to communicate between the 33 men and the surface was not smooth. While family members and the miners were allowed to exchange letters, their letters were read by a team of psychologists before they were delivered. The fear was that too much stress on the miners from letters that might discuss family controversies or conflicts might upset the group and bring down morale. The miners quickly became aware that their communications were being censored. Feeling patronized and controlled by psychologist Albert Iturra, the men reached such a point of anger that Iturra was asked to leave. Miner Carlos Barrios said of the officials, "They thought we were ignorant. They never understood us."[5]

Conditions in the mine were still difficult with a temperature of 95 degrees Fahrenheit (35°C) and

A Matter of Trust

Not all mental health experts agreed with censoring the letters to the miners. Nick Kanas, a professor of psychiatry and an adviser to NASA, the US space agency, was one of those critics. "I would not screen anything . . . otherwise you are setting up a basis for mistrust. The miners will start asking, 'What else are they hiding from us?' They will know they are not getting the full story and will want to know why."[6]

humidity that ranged from 80 to 95 percent. There was no UV light to kill bacteria and viruses, so many men suffered from infections. There was still a long road to travel before the miners could hope to be rescued, and it was not going to be smooth or easy.

Morale

Once it was confirmed that the miners were alive, the mood above and below ground changed. It was important for the miners to keep a positive attitude. Initially, the rescuers made the decision not to let the miners know that the rescue might not occur until December.

This decision was changed. Three days later, the miners learned of the scope of the rescue operation and a projected rescue deadline late in December. Used to working in the mines, the trapped men were given tasks to help with the rescue. This not only contributed to the progress but kept the men motivated and optimistic.

Photos and memorabilia of miner Yonni Barrios
were placed at the mine site.

This is a portion of the Schramm T-130 drill unit that became Plan B.

Plan B

The miners had been located, Plan A was underway, and the world waited for more news. Brandon Fisher, president of Center Rock Inc. in Berlin, Pennsylvania, wondered why officials thought four months was an acceptable amount of time to rescue the miners. Fisher's company designed, built, and delivered drilling systems. These systems differed from regular drilling units because the machinery used pneumatic hammers to smash through rock instead of drilling through it. This system was also an excellent choice for the San José mine. The hard volcanic rock was infused with other hard and brittle minerals, which made Fisher's drill an excellent option. With experience on other mining rescues, Fisher felt he could help the San José miners.

Fisher arrived at the mine on day 29, September 4. He had arranged with a US-Chile mining company to locate and deliver a Schramm T-130 drill unit to the San José mine. This drill became Plan B. But the drill rig needed modifications to be used at this mine. Usually, it drilled blind, meaning there was no way to guide it. Fisher's factory in Pennsylvania would

Extra Pay

Dario Segovia's partner, Yessica Chilla, remembers Segovia told her something was going to happen. "The day before the accident, he told me the mine was about to settle and that he didn't want to be on shift when the collapse arrived. But we needed the money. His shift had ended, but then they offered him extra hours. No one refuses because they pay you double. That day he was going to earn ninety thousand pesos [$175]. But he wanted to leave this job to run a trucking business."[1]

make a special drill bit with a snout on the tip that would fit into the preexisting borehole, guiding the hammers on the correct course.

The drill had never been used to make such a deep hole. The engineers worried the drill bit might be too heavy for the drilling machine to pull back out of the ground when it was done. "One of the most important things when you drill is to know exactly what the drill is going to weigh," a Plan B engineer explained. "It is easy to go down, but you have to remember to be able to pull up everything."[2] In this case, 48 short tons (44 metric tons) of drilling shaft would have to be pulled out.

Hope

The 33 men trapped in the San José mine came from many different backgrounds and would be remembered for certain things that occurred while they were trapped. Miner Osmán Araya told his wife and baby daughter via video, "I will fight to the end to be with you."[3] Edison Peña became known as the song leader and requested Elvis Presley songs be sent into the mine. Peña ran in the open portions of the mine tunnels every day the men were trapped. The children of Omar Reygadas kept a video diary while they waited for his rescue. Esteban Rojas and his wife were married 25 years earlier in a civil ceremony. Now he told her he would marry her in a church once the miners were rescued. José Henriquez was a preacher who had worked in mining for more than 30 years and organized daily prayers for the trapped men. On September 14, 2010, miner Ariel Ticona, the communication specialist in the group, watched the arrival of his baby daughter by video. He named her Esperanza, which means "hope."

Plan B required a great deal of drilling equipment. The Chilean Embassy in Washington DC convinced the United Parcel Service (UPS), a shipping company, to put together the massive rush shipment of 13.5 short tons (12.2 metric tons) of drilling equipment. The UPS Foundation, a philanthropic division of UPS, paid for the shipping.

With a new plan and equipment on the way, the Plan B team also needed a man to guide the drill and serve as leader. Jeff Hart, an expert driller, was drilling water wells in Afghanistan for the US Army. Known to be the best at handling the T-130 and working in difficult situations and environments, Hart was selected to lead the drilling operation and was flown to Chile. Recognizing the many challenges of Plan B, and the 33 men whose lives depended on him, he began drilling on September 5.

Safety Issue

As the drill rotated, the rock was hammered and crushed. The initial intent was to use compressed air to move the cuttings upward. But due to safety concerns, this process was not used. Instead, with the approval of the Chilean Mining Agency, the cuttings were allowed to fall down in the mine. The miners were given the job of removing the cuttings from their refuge.

Working Together and Facing Obstacles

With both Plan A and Plan B underway, a friendly competition developed between the teams to see who would reach the miners first. In reality, this was a race with just one team comprised of several competing mining companies, each wanting at least one of the plans to succeed.

By day 35, September 9, Plan A slowly chewed its way through the rock. It had already reached 490 feet (149 m). Plan B was faster. Drilling a small hole ten hours a day, Hart seldom left his station. However, additional drilling was required to widen the hole enough to accommodate a man.

The drilling business is risky and often frustrating. When the Plan B drill hit 879 feet (268 m), Hart realized the air pressure had collapsed. The drill was spinning but no longer cutting into the rock. Unable to determine the cause, the Plan B engineers had to stop drilling and pull the drill out of the hole.

The evidence was obvious: the drill head was shredded. Football-sized chunks had been torn off the tungsten-steel shaft. A video camera that was lowered down the hole revealed the missing pieces had become entangled with iron.

An engineer and deputy chief of the rescue operations, Rene Aguilar, held part of the broken hammer of the Plan B T-130 drill.

Faulty maps had led the engineers to design a drilling route that passed through a layer of rods used to reinforce the mine. Now those rods had sabotaged the rescue tunnel.[4]

ANOTHER SETBACK

Plan B was stalled. On September 10, mining engineers tried several methods to get the metal chunks out of the way. They lowered huge magnets through the shaft, but these did not pick up the pieces. Next, they tried hammering the shards, hoping to loosen them from the rock, but that did not work.

Chilean engineer Igor Proestakis suggested a possible solution. He designed an open metal jaw with teeth-like edges that could be lowered into the shaft to surround the fragments. Huge amounts of pressure would begin to close the jaws, hopefully encasing the fragments, snap shut, and bring the fragments up to the surface. This was a very old mining technique known as *la Araña*, "the spider."

This technique was so simple and old-fashioned that the engineer could not convince the rescue leaders

Safety

Mario Sepulveda had tried to organize his fellow miners to join the workers' trade union Central Unitaria de Trabajadores because of the safety violations in the mine. He gave up when he thought the union was only interested in what mine owners wanted it to do rather than defending its workers.

to try it. For the moment, Plan B was going nowhere, and its drill and fragments blocked one of the three precious boreholes linking the 33 men to the surface.

There was more bad news that day. Plan A developed a problem. The drill had a leaking hydraulic hose. Work had to be stopped to make repairs. Deep inside the mine, the 33 men realized all sounds of drilling—and potential rescue—had suddenly stopped. The silence was frightening.

THE SPIDER SAVES THE DAY

On September 12, Proestakis convinced rescue officials to give his idea a try. Fisher said, "We quickly started to manufacture an on-site fishing tool apparatus to go down and retrieve the broken metal out of the ground."[5] The spider was built at the site by Fisher's men and sent down through the shaft. Pressure from above

Money and Lives

Raul Dagnino is the director of a drilling company that helped in the rescue. In an interview for NOVA, he said, "When you are in the drilling business, you know, you drill a hole and if you lose a hole you lose money. But if you lose the holes here you can lose lives."[6]

forced the teeth inward. As the spider was reeled back up, the engineers waited for the moment of truth:

> *At the surface, a metalworker with a blowtorch cut into the Spider's cocoon, slicing away the teeth one by one. In a spray of sparks, he removed the final tooth and out rolled the Spider's catch: a tungsten hammerhead.* [7]

On September 14, Plan B was back in action, but the rescue teams were worried. For a time, both plans had been out of action. Many feared the miners might never be rescued. Clearly, a third plan was required to ensure a successful rescue.

One Bolivian

Bolivian Carlos Mamani was the only man trapped in the mine who was not Chilean. The day of the collapse was his first day of work in the mine. He had decided to work a second job at the San José mine because he had a new baby to support.

Chile and Bolivia had hundreds of years of bad feelings between their countries, and it was especially challenging for him to be caught underground with 32 Chileans. Mamani later declined an offer from Bolivia's president to accept a job in his home country due to its poor working conditions and inadequate housing.

Using the Plan B drill, the rescue efforts continued.

Plan C was underway with a drill donated by Precision Drilling.

PLAN C

iner Victor Segovia's letter to his brother on the surface reflected the grim atmosphere in the San José mine, "There is no way I'm going to lie to you . . . . This hell is killing me. I try to be strong, but it's difficult."[1] The miners knew all activity had stopped and wondered if their rescue was in jeopardy.

As part of Plan C, the third plan, the first of a convoy of 42 trucks had rolled through the mine gates on September 11. The trucks were loaded with towers, tubes, machinery, and generators used in petroleum drilling operations. The Plan C drill required a platform and could not be located directly above the miners. It would dig at an angle of 85 degrees to reach the miners' workshop. The arrival of yet another plan to free the miners came at just the right time when many of the miners and their families were losing hope.

A Setback

The Plan C drilling rig had been donated by Precision Drilling, a Canadian company that specializes in finding oil. It had been stored for several years in a warehouse approximately 1,000 miles (1,610 km)

Faith

The Chilean government asked Al Holland, a NASA psychologist, to work with the miners and their families. Holland explained how important faith was: "Faith plays a key role in maintaining your motivation to survive. It's that hope; it's the understanding of the people who are trying to rescue you, that they're technically good, that they are working 24/7 on your behalf; faith in your family that your family has not given up on you; faith in comrades that are with you, that they will keep encouraging you, and you will keep encouraging them; and faith in yourself and in your religion. And without those, they'd lose the ability as a team, to continue to work toward their survival."[2]

north of Copiapó. Once assembled, the drilling rig would stand 150 feet (46 m) tall and was expected to drill at a rate of 328 feet (100 m) a day. Shaun Robstad, the team leader for the company, said, "We're coming in to, hopefully, drill a well here, that's all, and pull them out."[3]

Setting up Plan C, however, was met with challenges. While the rig was in storage, thieves had broken into the warehouse and stolen whatever copper they could find on the rig. Copper was selling at a very high price, and the thieves stripped it from the rig cables and removed much of the circuitry in the process.

Recognizing this latest setback, Robstad admitted,

It was a little frustrating to come back to Chile. . . . Some electrical cables were stolen. All the cords were gone, so my electrician got on the phone and started ordering cable. It was all put together in Houston [Texas]. . . . A lot of people worked weekends and nights to get it done.[4]

Once more, people around the world pitched in to help 33 strangers. The rig was assembled in half of the expected time.

Things were looking better for the miners, but it was still difficult for the men and their families.

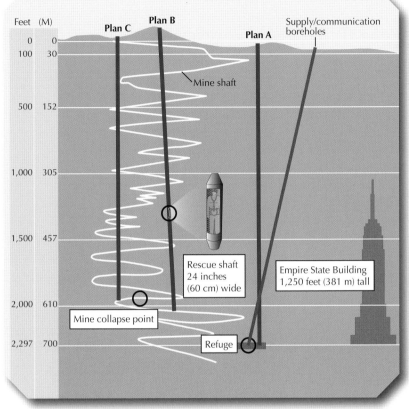

Feet	(M)				
		Plan C	Plan B	Plan A	Supply/communication boreholes
0	0				
100	30				
500	152			Mine shaft	
1,000	305				
1,500	457			Rescue shaft 24 inches (60 cm) wide	Empire State Building 1,250 feet (381 m) tall
2,000	610			Mine collapse point	
2,297	700			Refuge	

Three different drilling routes were used in the effort to rescue the miners.

It was now September 14, and the miners had been trapped underground for 40 days—15 days longer than anyone had been trapped underground. Families gathered to pray, hoping for the safe return of their men even as the rescue attempts stopped and started and stopped again.

DOWN IN THE MINE

It became more difficult in the mine as the days went by. The men had to deal with their garbage. They filled barrels with refuse and used the heavy machinery to carry the barrels to the lowest level of the mine. Without proper bathrooms, waste disposal was also a problem. The smell of urine wafted into their living area until the men began using empty water bottles to relieve themselves and put the bottles in the rubbish barrels.

Other problems arose. Initially, the men had kept a schedule of chores, but once they were given television to watch, many stopped doing the chores. "Some of the guys would just stare at it; they were hypnotized and watched it all day."[6]

Now that the miners were receiving food and other comforts daily, some of the hardship that had drawn the men together was fading. Pedro Gallo, the telephone technician on the surface who spoke with the men every day, described what happened:

> During the different shifts, the men would go around and check on those who were asleep. They would put their hand on the chest of every sleeping man to make sure he was breathing. Because of the carbon monoxide in the mine, they wanted to make sure he was alive. These were known as the "Guardian Angels". . . they were vigilant in protecting the men who were asleep, but when the TV began, they stopped doing the rounds . . . they preferred to watch television.[7]

Last Man Out

Several of the miners said they wanted to be the last man out of the mine. Rescuers quickly discovered why: the last man out would be guaranteed the slot in the *Guinness Book of World Records* for the longest time a miner had ever been trapped underground. The situation was resolved when Guinness World Records decided to award the record to the entire group of 33 miners rather than one individual.

The rescue work continued, however, and all three drilling plans were running. On the morning of day 43, September 17, the Plan B drill, which used one of the three exploratory holes, broke through the roof of an access tunnel close to the miners' workshop. This was a sorely needed milestone. Everyone, above and below ground, hoped the end was in sight. ⌐

Proven Wrong

Due to the lives of the 33 men at stake, both Fisher and Hart acknowledged drilling in the San José mine was the most difficult they had ever experienced. Many experts thought the rescue effort was an impossible task. Fortunately, they were proven wrong.

The Plan C drill was fast and made a hole wide enough to pull a man out.

*Golborne, left, the mining minister, and Sougarret,
head of the rescue operation, updated the families and media.*

BREAKTHROUGH

reaking through to the mine on
September 17, day 43, was a milestone.
The next task in Plan B was to enlarge the shaft to
allow the men to be pulled through it and brought
to the surface.

Fisher's Pennsylvania factory created a new drill to widen the shaft from 12 inches (30 cm) to 28 inches (71 cm). The drill was made of four hammerheads that pounded the ground 20 times per second, widening the shaft at a rate of three feet per hour (.9 m/h). If nothing went wrong, they anticipated finishing the hole and rescuing the miners in 26 days.

September 18 was a day of celebration for the miners and their families. It was also Chilean Independence Day, honoring 200 years of independence. In a flat area where press conferences were usually held, the commander of Chile's submarine fleet held a ceremony to raise the Chilean flag. A banner with pictures of the 33 men was strung up near the flagpole and fluttered in the breeze.

The miners had their own small celebration. They were sent

Frozen Assets

A lawsuit had been filed against the San Esteban Mining Company before the rescue. A judge froze the company's assets, reportedly worth $2 million, which meant the company could not do anything with that money until the suit was settled. Lawyers for the miners' families were quick to point out the company claimed it did not have enough money to pay the miners' salaries but had $2 million in assets. As of April 2011, this lawsuit had not been settled and others are impending.

traditional food—empanadas, a type of stuffed bread or pastry—but the medical team did not allow red wine, which traditionally was part of the meal. The medical authorities on the surface, however, gave in to the men's request for cigarettes. Although other medical experts disagreed with the decision, one of the psychologists said that a stressful time was not a good opportunity for forcing those who smoked to quit. On a video transmission to the surface, Mario Sepulveda said,

Thank you to all our dear colleagues who

Expertise

Chile had reached out to NASA for its expertise. NASA makes the decision on who is selected for the US space program. Most of the men and women selected have not experienced long, stressful amounts of time alone. Accustomed to preparing astronauts for periods of isolation, the US agency offered advice gathered from the diverse experiences of those who had traveled through space in capsules—some of which malfunctioned. NASA also drew on the experiences of men who had been held captive in prisoner of war camps.

Most important, rescuers should be careful of not promising too much or raising expectations that might fall through. Research showed it was important for those who were isolated to have some privacy, although no one should be allowed to become a loner. Similarly, friendships are important, and no one should feel left out. By keeping to a regular sleeping schedule, the men could avoid fatigue, which could lead to poor decisions. Of equal importance was the feeling of purpose, which could be met by sharing in the work. Simple chores such as keeping the main area clean can make a trapped person feel productive. Exercise not only strengthened the men for their eventual rescue, but it also helped reduce stress.

have worked so hard for us. We are full of emotion for what's been achieved. And with this we want to thank you . . . with all our hearts![1]

An Unpleasant Surprise

Plan C drilling began on September 19, but on September 22, a problem arose with Plan B. When the drill bit reached 280 feet (85 m), it suddenly snapped and one of the four drill heads fell into the shaft. It hit the floor of the mine and buried itself in the mud. Fortunately, no one was hurt. But once again, Plan B was stopped.

Moments later, the telephone rang on the surface. Sepulveda said, "Ah, I think we have something of yours down here. I believe it is called a bit, a drill bit. But what is it doing here?"[2] He was attempting to joke, but his humor could not deny there was another setback.

A Setback

Regarding the drill bit that snapped off, Fisher later commented in an interview,

"Instantly they [the miners] were on the telephone. Called us to let us know there was a bit in the hole. The only time in my life that I've ever drilled a hole that we have communication below that tells us what's going on."[3]

Despite Sepulveda's joke, the miners were discouraged. One miner said,

> They are working to rescue you and you have this kind of failure? It was depressing. It means two more days—five more days. We were receiving food . . . but we were confined. Trapped! That was killing us.[4]

THE *FÉNIX* ARRIVES

While Fisher and his Plan B team worked to fix the drill head and resume widening the tunnel, there was another sign of hope for the miners. The *Fénix*, "Phoenix," which was the name of the rescue capsule that would bring the men to the surface through the shaft, arrived on site on September 25. Shaped like a missile, it had been built by the Chilean navy using specifications from NASA and from another successful mine rescue.

Painted in red, white, and blue, the colors of the Chilean flag, the *Fénix* weighed approximately 900 pounds (408 kg) and was only 21 inches (53 cm) in diameter. The inside chamber was 6.5 feet (2 m) high with oxygen tanks and a mesh door for ventilation. It had a mechanism that would split the capsule into two parts. If the capsule

This large winch was used to lower and hoist the rescue capsule.

jammed halfway up the shaft, the man inside could winch himself back down into the mine. As the capsule was unloaded, officials posed next to it for photographers, and family members touched it almost reverently, knowing it would bring their men back to them.

The arrival of the capsule also meant the 33 men needed to start preparing for their ascent through the more than 2,000 feet (610 m) of tunnel. They also had to be ready if something unexpected happened, such as the capsule jamming or failing, which might mean hauling the men up using only a cable. The men were told to start doing light exercises and jogging through a long stretch of tunnel that had been their home for weeks. The trapped miners were enthusiastic about their new regimen. As one of the doctors said,

> One of the advantages we have is that these guys are strong; they are accustomed to working their arms and upper bodies. This is not a sedentary population we are dealing with. They will respond quickly.[5]

Finally, all three drilling rigs were working. On October 1, Golborne spoke to the media and confirmed that the rescue effort was proceeding more quickly than had been publicly stated. He then added,

> The good news is that thanks to an analysis we have done together with the technical team, we can estimate that the rescue of our miners will happen in the second half of October.[6]

After 57 days, it seemed the rescue was finally in sight. ⌐

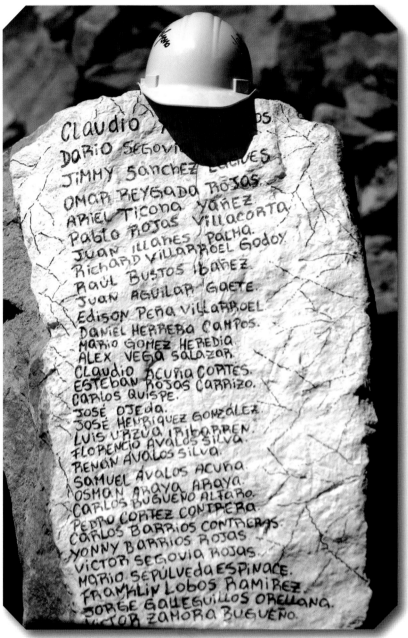

The names of the miners trapped
in the San José mine were inscribed on a rock.

*On September 29, Sougarret, center, explained
that it would take more weeks of drilling to reach the trapped miners.*

CLOSING IN

On day 65, October 9, with the Plan B drill closing in on the miners, the decision was made to shut down Plan A. It had never completed drilling a pilot hole. Authorities decided to focus on the other two plans. Plan B was close, and Plan C could serve as a backup. Plan C had become somewhat of a disappointment. The rock was harder than the rescuers thought. Drill heads had to be replaced every 20 hours—a process that took 12 hours to complete.

Putting the Miners to Work

In anticipation of a rescue within a few days, the miners were put to work. They needed to clear the buildup of debris from Plan B, which had accumulated on the floor of the tunnel. Engineer Rene Aguilar explained the situation:

> *The miners are working on Plan B every day. They work on shifts, three shifts, eight hours each shift. We need them to take out the work [waste rock and other materials from the shaft] that we are putting down with the drilling process. We are talking about almost 20 tons each day. . . . they use a charger, and they took*

In Preparation

Due to the limited size of the rescue capsule, the miners had exercised and were on a liquids-only diet. In addition to the custom-made jumpsuits and the monitors, the miners needed two more pieces of specialized equipment to make the journey to the surface in the rescue capsule. Each man wore a stomach girdle to reduce the effect of the pressure changes they would experience during the ascent. They also wore special thigh-high socks, similar to surgical stockings, to help their blood circulation. The men were given sunglasses to protect their retinas when they reached the surface after their lengthy period of living in the dark.

all the material and put it into a gallery which is 200 meters distance from the place that the material is going down.[1]

Officials, however, still refused to give the miners a firm date for their rescue. Too many things could go wrong. The tunnel had some slight curves and dips where the drill had occasionally gone off course and been corrected. Officials wondered if the *Fénix* capsule could negotiate these areas without getting stuck. It was necessary to use dynamite to expand the place where the shaft opened into the tunnel, which caused a concern that the shaft might collapse. Finally, the section of the shaft closest to the surface, where the rock was weakest, had to be reinforced with a steel tube lining.

PRACTICE MAKES PERFECT

The rescue team practiced winching the *Fénix* up and down

A Story to Be Told

Before the men were even rescued, talent scouts and television producers were already moving through Camp Hope, fighting to get the rights to the miners' life stories. Victor Segovia was known to be keeping a journal of his experiences underground. Publishing houses were already fighting over it, offering more than $25,000 for the rights to publish it. Tabloids tried to get the rights to first interviews with the various men, offering their families money and free trips. A movie was also in the works, even though none of the details of life underground were known yet.

Steel pipes were inserted into the escape tunnel to reinforce it.

within a section of the steel liner. They determined the rescue would take 20 minutes each way plus time for loading and unloading each miner.

On day 65, October 9, the rescuers informed the miners the drill was now only 33 feet (10 m) from the tunnel. Sepulveda sent a return message: "We are all going up the tunnel to watch the drill. When it comes through, we are going to dance and party all night."[2]

The men could hear the hammers of the drill pounding, and a steady stream of mud and water flowed onto the tunnel floor. One of the miners, Alex Vega, began writing a moment-by-moment account. Other miners provided updates to Hart, the driller, who adjusted the speed and pressure of the drill accordingly.

There was nothing to do but wait. The men heard the drill scream as it went through the tangled metal that had broken the drill hammer on its first pass. The drill jammed momentarily before starting to chew through the bolts in the tunnel ceiling.

"This is an important achievement, but we still have not rescued anybody. This rescue won't be over until the last person leaves the mine."[3]
—*Laurence Golborne, Chile's minister of mining*

Hart slowed the drill for the final few inches:

If he advanced too fast, the drill might pass straight through the roof and become jammed; wrenching the bit loose might shatter the fragile sections of the tunnel. . . . This time the drill overpowered the bolts and at 8 am, it broke through.

As the nub of the drill appeared through the roof of the workshop, a massive cloud of dust filled the caverns. Many of the men had a flashback to the first cave-in, as the dust cut off their vision. Now the dust storm was a glorious sign of freedom.[4]

Suddenly, the Plan B platform was filled with workers jumping and hugging each other, dancing, and making noise.

Surviving the Media

The world was waiting to hear the stories of the 33 men. While most of the media reported the facts, some reporters looked for scandalous and less noble stories. Tabloids hounded family members and bought letters, trying to find hints of scandal.

Hernán Rivera Letelier, a writer and former miner, tried to warn the men about what would happen next. He wrote,

I hope that the avalanche of lights and camera flashes rushing towards you is a light one. It is true that you have survived a long season in hell, but when all is said and done, it was a hell you know. What is heading your way, companions, is a hell that you have not experienced at all: the hell of the show, the alienating hell of TV sets. I have only got one thing to say to you, my friends: grab hold of your family. Don't let them go, don't let them out of your sight, don't waste them. Hold on to them as you hung on to the capsule that brought you out. It's the only way to survive the media deluge that is raining down on you.[5]

A Cooperative Success

The rescue team was comprised of various personnel, including drilling and technology experts, doctors, and NASA experts. Those who offered their help came from countries such as Canada, the United States, Germany, Japan, South Korea, and Australia. Estimates for the cost of the rescue range from $10 to $20 million. But the bottom line is the hope that more and better safety measures are implemented in the mining industry—measures that could prevent a similar event from happening in the future.

Sirens blared as bells and horns rang through the air. After two months, the rescue team had finally reached the miners. Hart said, "Two days ago we sent [the miners] a message: 'We will be there.' Now I would say, 'Follow us!'"[6] He continued by stating,

> We finally got there, we fought all this time. We have an avenue now that we can actually rescue these miners. . . . There's nothing more important that I will ever do.[7]

Family members of the miners surrounded Hart, hugging him and asking him to pose for photographs. Instead, he and his Plan B team quietly packed up and left the San José mine, not waiting to view the rescue that would take place. "I want to let this become the miners' and their families' story and let them have their time," Hart said.[8]

Relatives of the trapped miners awaited the rescue of the first miner.

Mãnalich, Chile's health minister, looked over the rescue capsule.

Day 69

On day 66, October 10, the miners awoke at 6:00 a.m. to the roar of the mountain around them. Dust and a strange wind blew through the tunnels. The men were convinced that another collapse was about to occur. Samuel Avalos said,

"I thought we were doomed. This whole thing is coming down. If it does, we are gone. The whole mountain was unstable. Anything could happen."[1] Sougarret let the men know there was a collapse in a different part of the mountain, but they were not in danger. By noontime, most of the cracking noise had subsided, but the miners remained uneasy, wondering if the mountain would collapse at any moment.

On day 67, the miners began to get the area beneath the shaft ready for their rescue and surrounded it with spotlights. Rescuers sent down custom-made waterproof jumpsuits for each of the 33 men to wear in the rescue capsule. The men also received sunglasses to protect their eyes from the bright lights after more than two months in darkness.

At 3:00 p.m., the miners had one last job to accomplish. Because the rescue capsule was too wide, it could

Testing the *Fénix*

The engineers working on rescuing the miners had to be sure the rescue capsule was safe before they started bringing the miners up. On October 11, the *Fénix* capsule was sent 2,000 feet (610 m) into the rescue hole, almost 40 feet (12 m) short of entering the mine's tunnel system. According to Golborne, the capsule did not loosen any dust in the hole. He also said, "We didn't send it [all the way] down because we could [not] risk that someone will jump in."[2]

not descend low enough into the tunnel to enable the men to climb inside without the capsule getting stuck on one of the walls. The miners were asked to place explosives to open up the narrow section of the rock wall. It was a routine task for any miner, and the men carried it out successfully. The mountain, however, once again shifted ominously following the blast. Loose rocks slid inside the tunnel. The lowest level of the mine, where the men had taken their refuse, collapsed. But the shaft held, and the mountain quieted.

Once the last adjustments were made to the *Fénix* capsule, it was loaded with 176 pounds (80 kg) of sand to represent the weight of a man. The capsule was then lowered through the shaft to determine an approximate time for rescuing each man. At 7:00 p.m. on day 68, October 12, Sougarret sent a Twitter message that the men "have spent

Mixed Emotions

Villarroel took a series of photographs of the place where the miners had spent their 69 long days underground. He took photographs of the refuge, his bed, and his friends smiling and posing for the camera. He photographed the walls of the refuge, which were decorated with flags and thank-you notes. He felt a sadness to be leaving his friends who were still below until the moment when he finally felt fresh air on his face and emerged from the capsule.

*Technicians positioned the capsule
for the rescue operation of the 33 trapped miners.*

their last night underground."[3] Everything was ready
for the rescue.

First Man Out

Rescuers had decided the first man to leave
the mine should be in relatively good shape. They
reasoned that if something unexpected happened, he
could winch himself out of the capsule. The assistant

foreman, Florencio Avalos, was selected as the first miner to be rescued by the *Fénix*. An experienced miner, he was in the best physical condition and could handle difficult situations.

Just after 11:00 p.m. on day 68, October 12, rescue specialist Manuel Gonzalez was strapped into the *Fénix*, which was then winched down into the shaft. Gonzales reached the tunnel, approximately 2,000 feet (610 m) deep, and greeted the miners. His job was to help each miner into the capsule and send it up. Avalos, with monitors on his wrists, hands, and chest to monitor his pulse and oxygen levels, entered the capsule. At 11:53 p.m., the door was latched shut, and the capsule ascended. Twenty minutes later, Avalos rose into the bright spotlights on the surface. As the capsule door opened and he was pulled out, his nine-year-old son, Byron, burst into tears and hugged his father. Sixty-nine days after the collapse of the San José mine, the first of the 33 men had been safely rescued.

Nick Evans, who blogged about the events at the San José mine for PBS television, remarked:

> *In the end, they made it all look so easy. After the nervous final moments of preparation, the delay caused by the last-*

minute trial runs . . . we at the camp and a billion viewers across the world breathed a sigh of relief with the emergence of the first miner from his subterranean prison.[4]

On the evening of day 69, October 13, the last of the 33 miners reached the surface. Amid the joy, the rescue had its moments of tension as more landslides and shifting made rescuers fear the shaft might not hold together long enough to get all the men out. The last trapped miner to leave the mine was Urzúa—the shift foreman credited with saving the lives of the men in the first few days of their confinement. Urzúa stepped out

Media Exposure

The miners made a pact before their rescue, promising each other they would limit what they would discuss with the media. They agreed to work together and appear together, sharing any money they earned. Knowing they would face incredible media exposure, and could possibly make a great deal of money telling their stories, the group wanted to ensure that each man would profit from the shared experience.

As expected, the 33 men who survived 69 days in the San José mine received many publicity and appearance requests. All 33 men and some of their rescuers appeared on CNN's *Heroes* special in November 2010. However, their media pact did not last long. The miners found it impossible to avoid media attention as individuals. Miners were invited to appear on the popular Spanish-language television show *Sabado Gigante* in Miami, Florida. Peña ran in the New York City marathon and appeared as a guest on the *Late Show with David Letterman* television program. An Elvis fan, Peña was also invited to visit Graceland, the music icon's famous home in Memphis, Tennessee, during Presley's birthday celebration in January 2011.

The Aftermath

Within days of the collapse, 18 Chilean mines were closed. The nation's mining regulatory agency plans to reorganize. Most important, the mine collapse brought attention to safety standards.

On October 17, 2010, as a way to bring their experience to a close, 12 of the 33 men returned to the San José mine. A mass was planned. Afterward, some of the miners explored the camp and viewed the borehole that had brought them to safety. Miner Samuel Avalos commented, "I found the hole very small. I still can't explain how I came out of that hole. If you ask me, I can't understand—without doubt it was a rebirth."[7] Some stood at the mouth of the mine and screamed insults at it, throwing rocks into the hole. The mine had attacked them, but they had won.

Due to economic and safety issues, the mine remains closed for the foreseeable future.

of the *Fénix* capsule and shook hands with Piñera. In the mining tradition of passing the responsibility for his men to someone else, he said, "Mr. President, my shift is over."[5] Rescuer Gonzalez was the last man to return to the surface.

For 69 days, the rescue effort had been watched throughout the world from the first news of the collapse to the moment when Urzúa stepped from the capsule. The rescue was possible because people across the world helped. These included workers who built and shipped drill bits, volunteers at Camp Hope, and companies that donated millions of dollars of equipment and expertise. Journalist Franklin said, "The bravery of thirty-three men and a band of generous and tenacious rescue workers brought the world together. At least for a moment, we could all say, 'We are Chilean.'"[6]

Urzúa, the last miner to be rescued, was greeted with a hug from Piñera.

TIMELINE

August 5, 2010	August 5, 2010	August 5, 2010
At 11:30 a.m., the mountain in the Atacama Desert makes cracking sounds.	At 2:00 pm, the San José mine collapses and traps 33 men deep underground.	At 6:00 p.m., GOPE is notified of the situation.

August 22, 2010	August 22, 2010	August 23, 2010
A note that the 33 men are alive is attached to a drill bit and sent to rescuers above ground.	The first video images of the miners are made.	Supplies are sent to the miners through the borehole.

August 7, 2010

Heavy drilling machinery triggers another collapse.

August 9, 2010

André Sougarret becomes general manager of the rescue effort.

August 19, 2010

The first borehole reaches an area where the miners are believed to be trapped.

August 23, 2010

A fiber optic cable allows the miners to communicate with the rescue team.

August 31, 2010

Plan A drilling begins.

September 4, 2010

US drilling executive Brandon Fisher arrives at the mine site to aid in the rescue.

TIMELINE

September 5, 2010	September 9, 2010	September 14, 2010
Plan B drilling begins.	The Plan B drill head no longer cuts into the rock.	Plan B drilling resumes.

September 24, 2010	September 25, 2010	October 9, 2010
The miners have been trapped for 50 days, longer than anyone else in history.	The *Fénix* rescue capsule arrives on site.	The repaired Plan B drill breaks through into the underground workshop.

September 17, 2010

Plan B reaches an access tunnel close to the trapped miners.

September 19, 2010

Plan C drilling begins.

September 22, 2010

The Plan B drill bit snaps and a drill head falls into the shaft.

October 11, 2010

Testing of the *Fénix* rescue capsule begins.

October 12, 2010

The rescue capsule is lowered to the 33 men late at night.

October 13, 2010

All 33 men are brought to the surface.

Essential Facts

Date of Event

August 5, 2010, to October 13, 2010

Place of Event

The San José mine in northern Chile, South America

Key Players

- ❖ 33 trapped miners
- ❖ Sebastián Piñera, Chilean president
- ❖ Laurence Golborne, Chilean minister of mining
- ❖ André Sougarret, rescue operations manager
- ❖ Chilean Carabineros Special Operations Group
- ❖ Greg Hall, mining expert
- ❖ Jeff Hart, expert driller
- ❖ Brandon Fisher, president of a company that creates drilling systems

Highlights of Event

- ❖ On August 5, 2010, a section of tunnel in the San José mine collapsed and trapped 33 miners.
- ❖ Contact was made with the men on August 22 and verified all of the men were alive.
- ❖ Boreholes were drilled to supply the men with liquids, nutrients, and medicines.

- On day 26, August 31, 2010, Plan A began by using a Strata drilling machine. It could drill a hole as deep as two miles (3.2 km); however, it would take approximately four months to finish the rescue tunnel.

- Fisher suggested using pneumatic hammers to speed up the rescue process. Plan B began on September 5.

- On September 9, the Plan B drill was spinning, but it no longer cut into the rock. Plan B engineers pulled the drill out for repairs.

- On September 10, the Plan A drill had a leaking hydraulic hose. Drilling was temporarily stopped to make repairs. The trapped miners realized all sounds of drilling—and potential rescue—had stopped.

- Plan C drilling began on September 19.

- On September 25, the *Fénix* rescue capsule arrived.

- By day 62, October 6, the Plan B drill was closing in on the miners.

- The rescue hole reached the men on October 9.

- Just after 11:00 p.m. on day 68, October 12, rescue specialist Gonzalez was strapped into the *Fénix* and winched down into the tunnel. He would help each miner into the capsule and send it up. Florencio Avalos was the first miner to be rescued.

- On day 69, October 13, the last of the miners, shift foreman Urzúa, reached the surface.

QUOTE

"Estamos Bien En El Refugio los 33." (We are all right in the shelter, the 33 of us.)—*note pinned to end of drill bit, proving the 33 men were still alive, August 22, 2010*

GLOSSARY

bit
> A device attached to the end of the drill that bores or cuts into material such as rock.

borehole
> A hole drilled into the earth, usually to extract a sample of rock.

carbon monoxide
> A colorless and odorless toxic gas.

compounded
> To make greater.

diplomatic
> Tactful, especially in difficult situations.

fiber optics
> Transmitting light through transparent fibers to transmit images or data.

foreman
> The person in charge of a particular department or group of workers.

glucose
> A type of sugar found in foods and in human and animal tissues.

hydraulic
> Operated or moved by water.

impending
> Something that is about to occur.

paparazzi
> Freelance photographers who pursue celebrities.

paramedic
> A medical technician trained for emergency situations.

percussion drill
> A tool that operates by hammering or hitting a surface rather than grinding it.

perforating
> Making a line of holes to facilitate separation.

pillar
> An upright shaft or structure used as a building support.

pneumatic
> Operated by air or air pressure.

respiratory
> Having to do with the lungs and breathing.

rig
> The equipment used for drilling an oil well.

shaft
> An enclosed passageway or vertical space.

shrine
> A small altar dedicated to a religious figure or used as a remembrance of a person.

vein
> A mass or large deposit of mineral found within rock.

ventilation
> Facilities or equipment for providing fresh air to an area.

winch
> A motor or hand-driven machine used for lifting or hauling.

windbreak
> A growth of trees or a landform that provides shelter from wind.

ADDITIONAL RESOURCES

SELECTED BIBLIOGRAPHY

Franklin, Jonathan. *33 Men: Inside the Miraculous Survival and Dramatic Rescue of the Chilean Miners.* New York: Putnam, 2011. Print.

Levin, David. "NOVA: Rescuing the Miners." *PBS.* WGBH Educational Foundation, 27 Oct. 2010. Web.

Parry, Wynne, and Rachael Rettner. "Chile Mine Collapse: Facts About the Amazing Survival Story." *MSNBC.* MSNBC.com, 27 Aug. 2010. Web.

FURTHER READINGS

Aronson, Marc. *Trapped: How the World Rescued 33 Miners from 2,000 Feet Below the Chilean Desert.* New York: Atheneum, 2011. Print.

DiPiazza, Francesca. *Chile in Pictures.* Danbury, CT: Twenty-First Century, 2007. Print.

Rutter, John, *Mining, Minerals and Metals.* North Mankato, MN: Smart Apple, 2009. Print.

Web Links

To learn more about the Chilean miners' rescue, visit ABDO Publishing Company online at **www.abdopublishing.com**. Web sites about the Chilean miners' rescue are featured on our Book Links page. These links are routinely monitored and updated to provide the most current information available.

Places to Visit

Queen Mine Tours
478 North Dart Road, Bisbee AZ, 85603
866-432-2071
http://www.queenminetour.com/history.php
After almost 100 years of production, the Bisbee mines closed in 1975. The mines produced more than 4 million short tons (3,628,739 metric tons) of copper as well as gold, silver, lead, and zinc. This small museum is an affiliate of the Smithsonian. The tour takes visitors deep into the old workings of the famous Queen Mine.

Quincy Historic Copper Mine and Museum
49750 US Highway 41, Hancock, MI 49930
906-482-3101
http://www.exploringthenorth.com/quincy/mine.html
This historic mine is on the Keweenaw Peninsula in the Upper Peninsula of Michigan. Surface and underground tours are offered of the copper mine.

Western Museum of Mining and Industry
225 North Gate Boulevard, Colorado Springs, CO 80921
800-752-6558
http://www.wmmi.org/
The museum depicts the history of mining through a variety of exhibits and guided tours.

Source Notes

Chapter 1. No Way Out

1. Jonathan Franklin. *33 Men: Inside the Miraculous Survival and Dramatic Rescue of the Chilean Miners*. New York: Putnam, 2011. Print. 16.

2. "How Er. Andre Sougarret Rescued The Chilean Miners." *crazyengineers.com*. CrazyEngineers, 2011. Web. 29 Jan. 2011.

3. Jonathan Franklin. *33 Men: Inside the Miraculous Survival and Dramatic Rescue of the Chilean Miners*. New York: Putnam, 2011. Print. 2.

Chapter 2. The San José Mine

1. Jonathan Franklin. *33 Men: Inside the Miraculous Survival and Dramatic Rescue of the Chilean Miners*. New York: Putnam, 2011. Print. 35.

2. Ibid. 10.

3. Ibid. 20.

4. Ibid. 17.

5. Ibid. 21.

Chapter 3. Is Anyone There?

1. Jonathan Franklin. *33 Men: Inside the Miraculous Survival and Dramatic Rescue of the Chilean Miners*. New York: Putnam, 2011. Print. 34.

2. Ibid. 37.

3. Ibid. 38.

4. Ibid. 46.

5. Ibid. 118.

Chapter 4. We Are Alive

1. Jonathan Franklin. *33 Men: Inside the Miraculous Survival and Dramatic Rescue of the Chilean Miners*. New York: Putnam, 2011. Print. 119.

2. David Levin. "NOVA: Rescuing the Miners." *PBS*. WGBH Educational Foundation, 27 Oct. 2010. Web. 11 Mar. 2011.

3. Jonathan Franklin. *33 Men: Inside the Miraculous Survival and Dramatic Rescue of the Chilean Miners*. New York: Putnam, 2011. Print. 124.

4. David Levin. "NOVA: Rescuing the Miners." *PBS*. WGBH Educational Foundation, 27 Oct. 2010. Web. 11 Mar. 2011.

5. Jonathan Franklin. *33 Men: Inside the Miraculous Survival and Dramatic Rescue of the Chilean Miners*. New York: Putnam, 2011. Print. 51.

6. Ibid. 129.

7. Ibid.

8. Ibid. 130.

9. Jonathan Franklin and Juan Forero. "Chile mine rescue: Miner tells of despair, fear, hunger as the days wore on." *azcentral. com*. Washington Post. 16 Oct. 2010. Web. 6 Apr. 2011.

10. Rory Carroll and Jonathan Franklin. "Chile miners: Rescued Foreman Luis Urzúa's First Interview." *guardian.co.uk*. Guardian News and Media Limited. 14 Oct. 2010. Web. 11 Mar. 2011.

Chapter 5. Plan A

1. Jonathan Franklin. *33 Men: Inside the Miraculous Survival and Dramatic Rescue of the Chilean Miners*. New York: Putnam, 2011. Print. 134.

2. Philip Sherwell. "Camp Hope families Wait in Chile's Atacama Desert for Trapped Miners." *Telegraph*. Telegraph Media Group Limited, 28 Aug 2010. Web. 3 Mar. 2010.

3. Jonathan Franklin. *33 Men: Inside the Miraculous Survival and Dramatic Rescue of the Chilean Miners*. New York: Putnam, 2011. Print. 153.

4. Ibid. 160.

5. Ibid. 153.

6. Ibid. 152.

Chapter 6. Plan B

1. Jonathan Franklin. *33 Men: Inside the Miraculous Survival and Dramatic Rescue of the Chilean Miners*. New York: Putnam, 2011. Print. 42.

2. Ibid. 167.

3. "Chilean Miners Rescue—Part 1." *guardian.co.uk*. Guardian News and Media Limited. 12 Oct. 2010. Web. 4 Mar. 2011.

4. Jonathan Franklin. *33 Men: Inside the Miraculous Survival and Dramatic Rescue of the Chilean Miners*. New York: Putnam, 2011. Print. 169–170.

Source Notes Continued

5. "NOVA: Emergency Mine Rescue." *PBS*. WGBH Educational Foundation, 26 Oct. 2010. Web. 4 Mar. 2011.

6. Ibid.

7. Jonathan Franklin. *33 Men: Inside the Miraculous Survival and Dramatic Rescue of the Chilean Miners*. New York: Putnam, 2011. Print. 173.

Chapter 7. Plan C

1. "NOVA: Emergency Mine Rescue." *PBS*. WGBH Educational Foundation, 26 Oct. 2010. Web. 4 Mar. 2011.

2. Ibid.

3. Ibid.

4. Jonathan Franklin. *33 Men: Inside the Miraculous Survival and Dramatic Rescue of the Chilean Miners*. New York: Putnam, 2011. Print. 172.

5. Ibid. 191.

6. Ibid. 176.

7. Ibid. 177.

Chapter 8. Breakthrough

1. NOVA: Emergency Mine Rescue." *PBS*. WGBH Educational Foundation, 26 Oct. 2010. Web. 4 Mar. 2011.

2. Jonathan Franklin. *33 Men: Inside the Miraculous Survival and Dramatic Rescue of the Chilean Miners*. New York: Putnam, 2011. Print. 193.

3. Ibid. 209.

4. NOVA: Emergency Mine Rescue." *PBS*. WGBH Educational Foundation, 26 Oct. 2010. Web. 4 Mar. 2011.

5. Jonathan Franklin. *33 Men: Inside the Miraculous Survival and Dramatic Rescue of the Chilean Miners*. New York: Putnam, 2011. Print. 194.

6. Ibid. 199.

Chapter 9. Closing In

1. NOVA: Emergency Mine Rescue." *PBS*. WGBH Educational Foundation, 26 Oct. 2010. Web. 4 Mar. 2011.

2. Jonathan Franklin. *33 Men: Inside the Miraculous Survival and Dramatic Rescue of the Chilean Miners*. New York: Putnam, 2011. Print. 224.

3. Ibid. 229.

4. Ibid. 226.

5. Ibid. 283.

6. Ibid. 228.

7. Cesar Iliano, "U.S. Drill Operator a Hero in Chile Mine Drama." *Reuters*. Thomson Reuters, 12 Oct. 2010. Web. 9 Mar. 2011.

8. "Arvada Man Played a Key Role in Miners' Rescue." *Gazette. com*. Freedom Communications, 12 Oct. 2010. Web. 9 Mar. 2011.

Chapter 10. Day 69

1. Jonathan Franklin. *33 Men: Inside the Miraculous Survival and Dramatic Rescue of the Chilean Miners*. New York: Putnam, 2011. Print. 230.

2. "Chilean Miners Rescue Capsule Works in Test," *CBCNews*. CBC, 11 Oct. 2010. Web. 9 Mar. 2011.

3. Jonathan Franklin. *33 Men: Inside the Miraculous Survival and Dramatic Rescue of the Chilean Miners*. New York: Putnam, 2011. Print. 246.

4. Nick Evans. "Hope Fulfilled." *PBS*. WGBH Educational Foundation, 17 Oct. 2010. Web. 7 Mar. 2011.

5. Jonathan Franklin. *33 Men: Inside the Miraculous Survival and Dramatic Rescue of the Chilean Miners*. New York: Putnam, 2011. Print. 277.

6. Ibid. 300.

7. Ibid. 293.

INDEX

Urzúa, Luiz, 38, 39, 40–42, 48, 93–94
Vega, Alex, 84
Villarroel, Richard, 35, 40, 90
morale, 51–52

NASA, 51, 65, 74, 76, 86
National Emergencies Office of the Interior Ministry, 10

oil drilling rig, 28, 30, 31–32, 55, 65–66, 78
open pit mine, 18, 47

Pacific Ocean, 8
Piñera, Sebastián, 12, 28, 49, 94
Pinilla, Carlos, 21
Pino, Alejandro, 68
Plan A, 48–50, 54, 58, 61, 80
    Strata 950, 48–49
Plan B, 55–58, 60–62, 70, 72, 75, 76, 80, 81, 84, 86
    Schramm T-130, 55–56, 58–59, 60–61, 70, 75, 76
Plan C, 65–66, 81
pneumatic drilling, 55
Precision Drilling, 65
Proestakis, Igor, 60, 61
    spider, 60, 61–62
psychologists, 51, 65, 74

Ramirez, Lillian, 7
refeeding syndrome, 45–46
refuge, 22, 40, 41, 49, 57, 90
Robstad, Shaun, 66

San Esteban Mining Company, 7, 10, 15, 17, 42, 73
Segura, Mario, 26, 27
Sougarret, André, 9, 28–30, 32, 89, 90

temperature, 20, 51
Toro, Ivan, 15

Villegas, José Luis, 27

About the Author

Marcia Amidon Lusted is the author of more than 50 books for young readers. She is also an assistant editor for six children's magazines, a writing instructor, and a musician. She lives in New Hampshire with her family.

Photo Credits

Martin Bernetti/AFP/Getty Images, cover, 3, 11; STR/AFP/ Getty Images, 6, 77, 96 (top) ; DigitalGlobe/Getty Images, 13; ClassicStock/Alamy, 14; Julio Etchart/Alamy, 19; Red Line Editorial, Inc., 23, 33, 67; Ariel Marinkovic/AFP/Getty Images, 24, 80, 97 (top) ; Santiago Llanquin/AP Images, 29; Hector Retamal/AP Images, 34; Hector Retamal/AFP/Getty Images, 37, 59, 96 (bottom), 98 (top); Roberto Candia/AP Images, 43, 46, 53, 63, 95, 97 (bottom), 99 (top); Chilean Government/ Handout/REUTERS, 44; Ivan Alvarado/AP Images, 54, 64; Aliosha Marquez/AP Images, 71, 72; Natacha Pisarenko/AP Images, 79; Jorge Saenz/AP Images, 83; LatinContent/Getty Images, 87; Hugo Infante/AP Images, 88, 99 (bottom) ; Rodrigo Arangua/ AFP/Getty Images, 91, 99 (bottom)

• 112 •